This easy-to-follow guide will help you learn Microsoft Teams without any confusion. Each feature is explained in simple steps, making it easy to understand and use.

Whether you're a student, a professional, or brand new to Microsoft Teams, this book will give you the confidence to navigate the platform with ease. You'll learn how to chat, collaborate, and stay organized—helping you work more efficiently in both your personal and professional life.

Table of Contents

Microsoft Teams

Chapter 1: Introduction to Microsoft Teams

1.1 Understanding Microsoft Teams – An Overview of Its Purpose and Functionality

Microsoft Teams is a communication and collaboration platform designed to help individuals, businesses, and educational institutions work together effectively. It combines chat, video conferencing, file sharing, and integration with Microsoft 365 applications into a single interface. The platform enables teams to collaborate in real time, whether they are working remotely or in the same office.

Key Functions of Microsoft Teams:

- **Chat and Messaging:** Allows instant messaging with individuals or groups, including rich text formatting, emojis, GIFs, and file attachments.
- **Video and Audio Calls:** Supports one-on-one and group calls, making virtual meetings seamless.
- **File Sharing and Collaboration:** Users can upload, share, and edit files within Teams, with real-time co-authoring capabilities.
- **Integration with Microsoft 365 Apps:** Works with applications like Word, Excel, PowerPoint, OneNote, and SharePoint.
- **Channels and Teams:** Organizes discussions into different channels for specific topics or projects.
- **Security and Compliance:** Offers enterprise-grade security, including multi-factor authentication and data encryption.

Key Features of Microsoft Teams

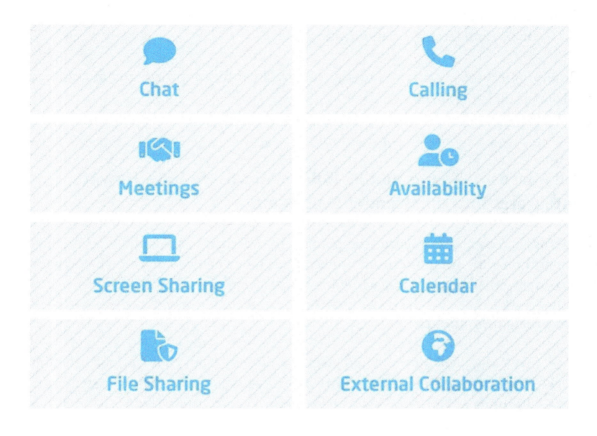

1.2 Benefits of Using Microsoft Teams – Why Businesses, Educators, and Individuals Rely on It

Microsoft Teams offers numerous benefits that enhance productivity and streamline communication. Its versatility makes it suitable for various industries, including businesses, schools, and personal projects.

Benefits for Different User Groups:

- **Businesses:** Improves teamwork through integrated communication tools, reducing reliance on multiple applications.

- **Educators:** Facilitates remote learning with virtual classrooms, assignments, and student engagement tools.
- **Individuals:** Provides a centralized space for managing projects, personal tasks, and family communications.

💡 **Tip:** Microsoft Teams reduces email overload by centralizing communication within a single platform.

1.3 Microsoft Teams and Its Role in Microsoft 365 – How It Integrates into the Broader Ecosystem

Microsoft Teams is a core component of Microsoft 365, allowing seamless integration with other Microsoft applications. Users can collaborate on documents directly from Teams without switching between apps.

Integration Highlights:

- **Outlook:** Schedule and join meetings directly from your Outlook calendar.
- **OneDrive & SharePoint:** Store and access shared files effortlessly.
- **Planner & To Do:** Manage tasks and projects within Teams.
- **Power Automate:** Automate repetitive tasks to improve efficiency.

1.4 Comparing Free and Paid Plans – Differences Between the Free Version, Business, Enterprise, and Education Editions

Microsoft Teams is available in multiple editions, catering to different user needs.

Feature	Free Plan	Business	Enterprise	Education
Chat & Meetings	✅	✅	✅	✅
File Storage	5GB	1TB per user	Unlimited	Unlimited
Meeting Duration	60 min	24 hours	24 hours	Custom
Integration with Office Apps	✖	✅	✅	✅
Security Features	Basic	Advanced	Enterprise-grade	Custom

💡 **Tip:** The free version is ideal for small teams, while business and enterprise plans offer enhanced security and collaboration features.

1.5 System Requirements for Installation – Minimum Hardware and Software Specifications

Before installing Microsoft Teams, ensure your device meets the minimum requirements.

Windows & Mac Requirements:

- **Processor:** 1.6 GHz or faster (dual-core recommended)
- **RAM:** 4GB minimum (8GB recommended)
- **Storage:** 3GB of available disk space
- **Operating System:** Windows 10 or later, macOS 10.14 or later
- **Internet Connection:** Broadband required

Mobile Requirements:

- **iOS:** iOS 13.0 or later
- **Android:** Android 8.0 or later

1.6 Installing Microsoft Teams – A Step-by-Step Guide

For Windows & Mac:

1. Visit the Microsoft Teams Download Page at https://www.microsoft.com/en/microsoft-teams/download-app
2. Click the **Download for desktop** button.
3. Open the downloaded file and follow the installation prompts.
4. Launch Teams and sign in.

For iOS & Android:

1. Open the App Store (iOS) or Google Play Store (Android).
2. Search for **Microsoft Teams** and tap **Install**.
3. Open the app and sign in with your Microsoft account.

1.7 Creating an Account and Signing In – How to Register and Log In

To use Microsoft Teams, you need a Microsoft account.

Creating an Account:

1. Go to Microsoft's Sign-Up Page at https://signup.live.com/
2. Click **Create Account** and enter your email or phone number.
3. Follow the prompts to complete registration.

Signing In:

1. Open Microsoft Teams.
2. Enter your email and password.
3. Choose **Stay signed in** for convenience (optional).

💡 **Tip:** If using a work or school account, your organization may have specific sign-in requirements.

Chapter 2: Navigating the Microsoft Teams Interface

2.1 Exploring the Home Dashboard – Understanding the Key Menus and Layout

Microsoft Teams provides a structured and organized home dashboard that serves as the main hub for communication, collaboration, and management of your workspace. Understanding the dashboard layout is essential for navigating the platform efficiently.

Key Components of the Home Dashboard:

1. **Top Navigation Bar:**
   - Displays the search bar for quick access to messages, files, and users.
   - Provides quick settings access and profile customization options.
   - Includes notification and activity indicators to alert users about updates.
2. **Left Navigation Panel:**
   - Houses primary tools such as Teams, Chats, Calendar, Calls, and Files.
   - Allows users to switch between different sections of Teams easily.
3. **Main Workspace Area:**
   - Displays the active content based on the selected tool (e.g., Chats, Meetings, or Teams channels).
   - Provides an intuitive layout for document collaboration, messaging, or video conferencing.
4. **Bottom Menu and Settings:**
   - Contains user settings, help center access, and logout options.

By understanding these elements, users can quickly adapt to Microsoft Teams and use its features effectively.

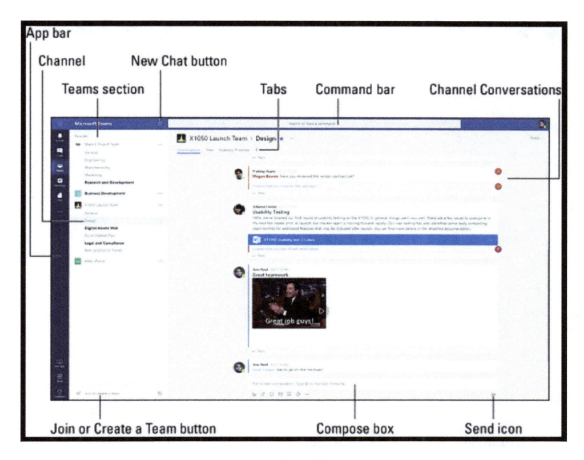

2.2 Personalizing Your Profile and Settings – Updating Your Display Name, Avatar, and Preferences

Customizing your profile in Microsoft Teams ensures that other users can recognize you easily, and it enhances your experience by tailoring the interface to your needs.

Steps to Personalize Your Profile:

1. **Accessing Profile Settings:**

- o Click on your profile picture or initials in the top right corner.
- o Select "Manage Account" to open the profile settings.

2. **Updating Your Display Name:**
   - o Navigate to the "General" tab.
   - o Click on "Edit Name" and enter the desired display name.
   - o Click "Save" to confirm changes.
3. **Changing Your Avatar (Profile Picture):**
   - o Click on your profile image and select "Change Picture."
   - o Upload an image from your device or choose an existing one.
   - o Click "Apply" to update your profile picture.
4. **Modifying Preferences:**
   - o Navigate to the "Settings" menu under "Manage Account."
   - o Adjust notification preferences, appearance settings, and language preferences.
   - o Save changes to customize your experience.

By personalizing your profile, you create a more engaging and professional presence in Microsoft Teams.

2.3 The Left Navigation Bar Explained – A Breakdown of Teams, Calendar, Calls, Chats, Files, and Apps

The left navigation bar is the primary tool for moving between different sections of Microsoft Teams. Understanding its components allows for efficient workflow management.

Components of the Left Navigation Bar:

1. **Activity:**
    o   Displays all notifications, mentions, and recent activities.

- o Helps users track updates within different teams and channels.
2. **Chat:**
   - o Provides access to one-on-one and group chats.
   - o Enables messaging, file sharing, and voice or video calls within chat conversations.
3. **Teams:**
   - o Shows a list of all teams the user is a part of.
   - o Allows users to access channels, discussions, and collaborative spaces.
4. **Calendar:**
   - o Integrates with Outlook to display scheduled meetings and events.
   - o Allows users to schedule and join Teams meetings.
5. **Calls:**
   - o Provides access to call history, voicemail, and dial pad (for users with calling capabilities).
   - o Enables direct calls to contacts within the organization.
6. **Files:**
   - o Centralized location for accessing shared files and documents.
   - o Syncs with OneDrive and SharePoint for seamless document management.
7. **Apps:**
   - o Enables integration with third-party apps and Microsoft 365 tools.
   - o Allows customization of Teams with additional functionalities.

By familiarizing yourself with these features, navigating Microsoft Teams becomes more intuitive and efficient.

2.4 Understanding the Activity Feed – How Mentions, Notifications, and Updates Work

The Activity Feed in Microsoft Teams helps users stay updated on messages, mentions, and other important events in their workspace.

How the Activity Feed Works:

1. **Locating the Activity Feed:**
   - Click on the "Activity" tab on the left navigation bar.

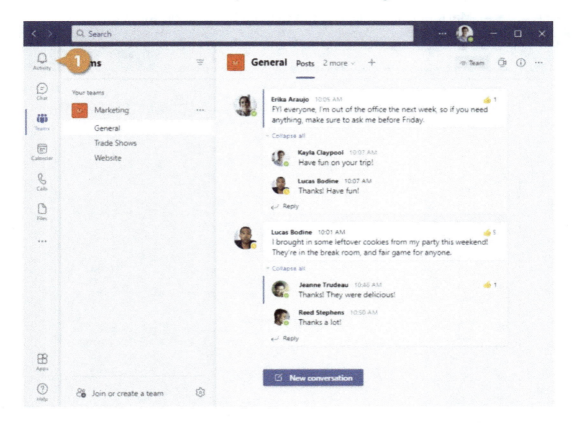

   - View a chronological list of recent activities, mentions, and notifications.
2. **Types of Notifications:**
   - **Mentions (@):** When someone tags you in a message or post.
   - **Replies:** Responses to your messages or conversations.
   - **Reactions:** Notifications when someone reacts to your message.
   - **Missed Calls and Voicemails:** Alerts for missed calls and voice messages.
3. **Filtering and Customizing Notifications:**
   - Click on the "Filter" icon to sort notifications by type.

- Adjust notification settings in "Manage Account" to control what triggers alerts.

4. **Clearing and Managing Notifications:**
   - Click on a notification to view the related message or activity.
   - Mark notifications as read to keep the feed organized.

The Activity Feed ensures users never miss important updates and can manage interactions efficiently.

2.5 Using Search and Commands – Finding Messages, Files, and People Efficiently

Microsoft Teams features a powerful search and command function that allows users to locate information quickly.

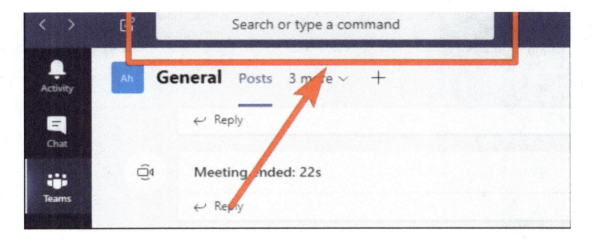

How to Use the Search Bar:

1. **Locating the Search Bar:**
   o Found at the top of the Teams interface.
   o Type keywords to search for messages, contacts, or files.
2. **Searching for Messages:**
   o Enter a keyword related to the conversation.
   o Use filters to narrow results by date, sender, or channel.
3. **Finding Files and Documents:**
   o Type the file name or a keyword related to the document.
   o Search results display recently shared files and storage locations.
4. **Searching for People:**
   o Enter a name or email address to locate a colleague.
   o Click on the result to start a chat or call.
5. **Using Command Shortcuts:**
   o **/call [Name]** – Quickly initiate a call.
   o **/chat [Name]** – Start a chat with a specific user.
   o **/files** – View recently shared files.
   o **/mentions** – See all messages where you were mentioned.

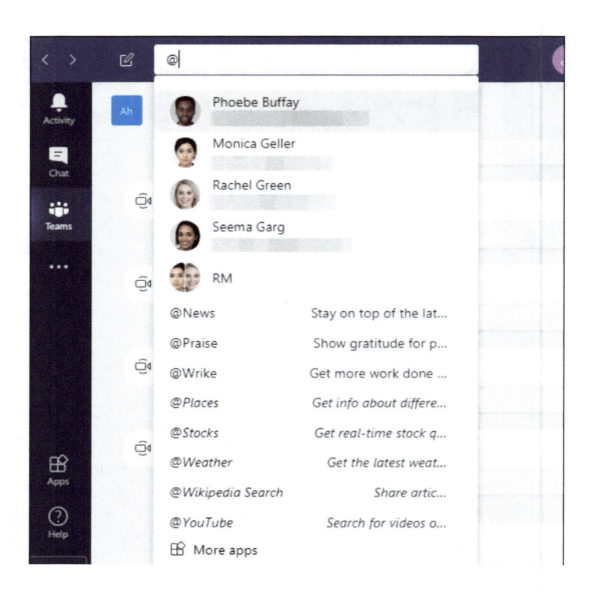

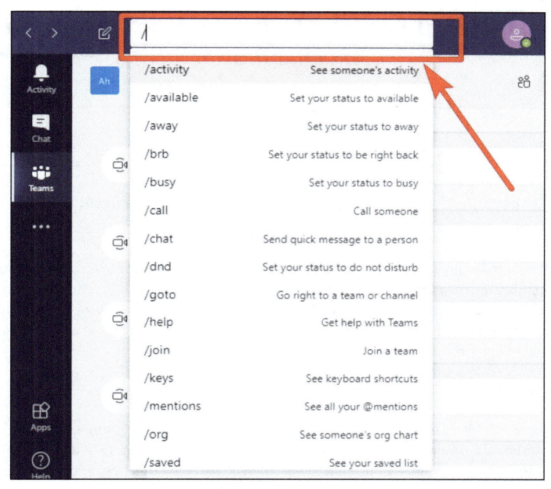

Type / to view the list of commands.

By leveraging search and command shortcuts, users can speed up workflow and find essential information without hassle.

Chapter 3: Teams and Channels – The Foundation of Collaboration

3.1 Introduction to Teams and Channels – Their Structure and Purpose

Microsoft Teams is designed to facilitate collaboration and communication within organizations, businesses, schools, and even personal groups. At its core, Teams is built around **Teams** and **Channels**, which help structure conversations, file sharing, and workflows in a logical way. Understanding these components is essential for maximizing productivity and ensuring seamless teamwork.

What Are Teams?

Teams in Microsoft Teams are **dedicated spaces where groups of people collaborate on specific tasks, projects, or topics**. Each Team includes multiple communication tools such as chat, file sharing, video conferencing, and integrated apps. Organizations create Teams based on **departments, projects, or functional groups**, ensuring focused discussions and resource sharing.

Key Features of Teams:

- Centralized communication hub.
- File and document storage via OneDrive and SharePoint.
- Integration with third-party applications.
- Secure collaboration within and outside the organization.

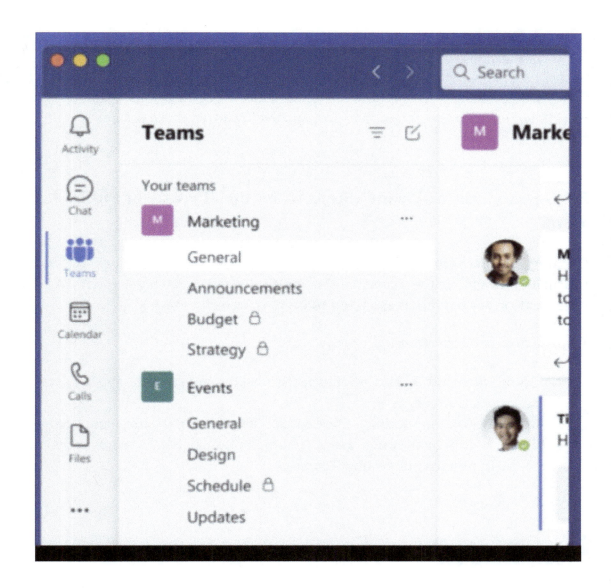

What Are Channels?

Channels are **subsections within a Team** that help organize conversations and files by topics, departments, or projects. Each Team **can have multiple Channels**, ensuring discussions remain focused and structured.

Types of Channels:

- **Standard Channels** – Open to all members within the Team.

- **Private Channels** – Restricted to specific members for confidential discussions.

Using well-organized Teams and Channels allows organizations to streamline workflows, ensure clear communication, and avoid cluttered discussions.

3.2 How to Create a Team – Steps to Set Up a Private or Public Team

Creating a Team in Microsoft Teams is a straightforward process that allows users to collaborate efficiently. Teams can be **public (open to everyone within the organization)** or **private (restricted to invited members only)**.

Steps to Create a New Team

1. **Open Microsoft Teams** – Launch the desktop app, mobile app, or access Teams via the web.
2. **Go to the Teams Section** – Click on the **Teams** tab in the left-hand sidebar.
3. **Click on 'Join or Create a Team'** – At the bottom of the Teams panel, you'll see an option to create a new Team.

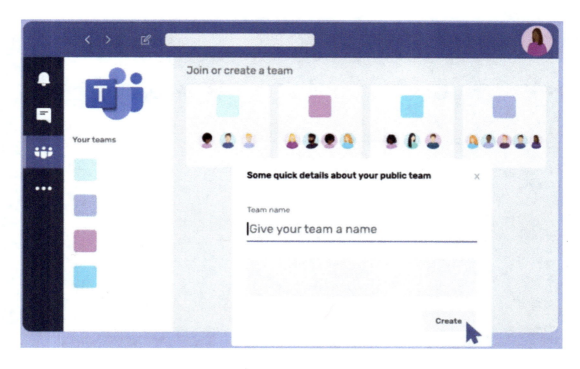

4. **Choose 'Create a Team'** – Select this option to begin the setup process.

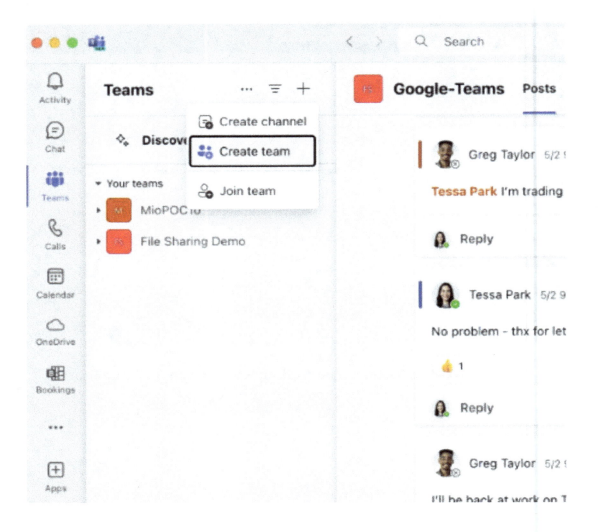

5. **Select the Type of Team**
   - ○ **From Scratch** – Build a new Team from the ground up.
   - ○ **From an Existing Microsoft 365 Group** – Use a pre-existing group from Microsoft 365.
6. **Set Privacy Settings**
   - ○ **Public** – Anyone in the organization can join.
   - ○ **Private** – Only invited users can join.

What kind of team will this be?

Privacy

Private
People need permission to join

Public
Anyone in your org can join

7. **Enter the Team Name and Description** – Choose a clear, descriptive name and an optional explanation of its purpose.

Create a team

You're creating a team from scratch. [More create team options](#)

Team name *

Give your team a name

Description

Let people know what this team is all about

8. **Add Members** – You can add individual users, groups, or even external guests.
9. **Click 'Create'** – Your new Team is now set up and ready to use.
10. **Customize Your Team** – Configure settings, add Channels, and integrate useful apps.

3.3 Managing Members and Roles – Adding, Removing, and Assigning Different Permissions

Once a Team is created, it is essential to manage members effectively to ensure smooth collaboration.

Roles in Microsoft Teams

1. **Owner** – The creator of the Team, with full control over settings, members, and content.
2. **Member** – Standard participant with access to Team resources.
3. **Guest** – External user with limited permissions.

Adding Members to a Team

1. Open the Team and click on the **three-dot menu** (More options).
2. Select **Manage Team** and click **Add Member**.

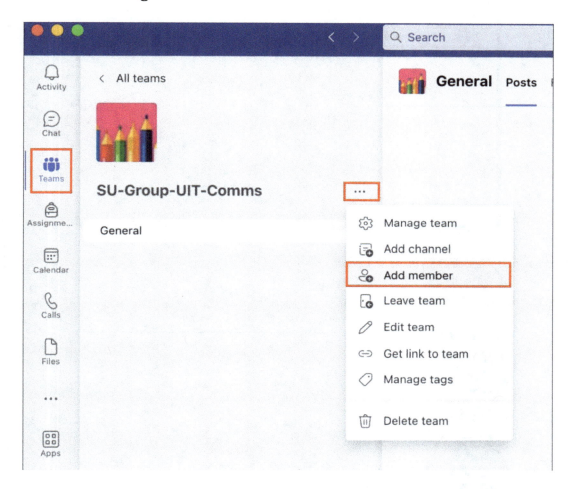

3. Enter the email address or username of the person you want to add.
4. Assign them a role (**Owner, Member, or Guest**).
5. Click **Add** to confirm.

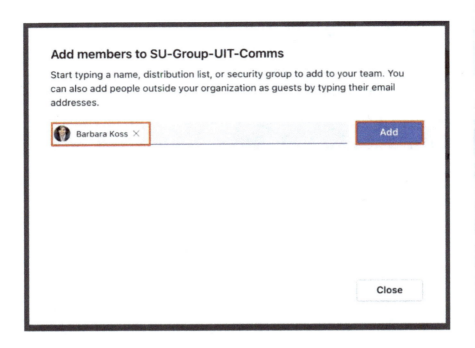

Removing Members from a Team

1. Navigate to **Manage Team**.

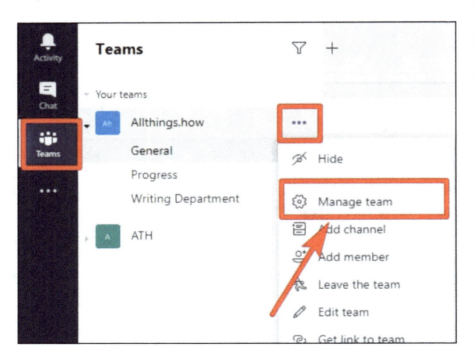

2. Locate the user under the **Members** list.

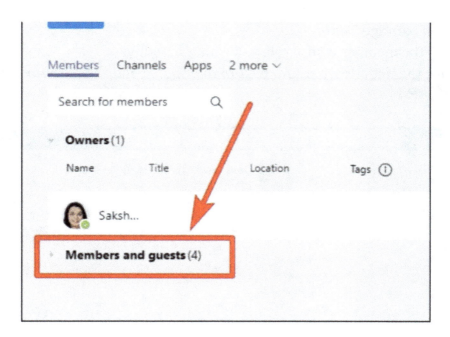

3. Click on the **Remove** button.

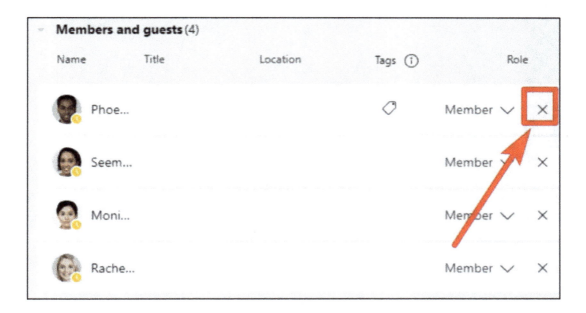

Changing Member Roles

1. Open **Manage Team**.
2. Find the member whose role you want to modify.
3. Click the **dropdown menu** next to their name and select **Owner, Member, or Guest**.

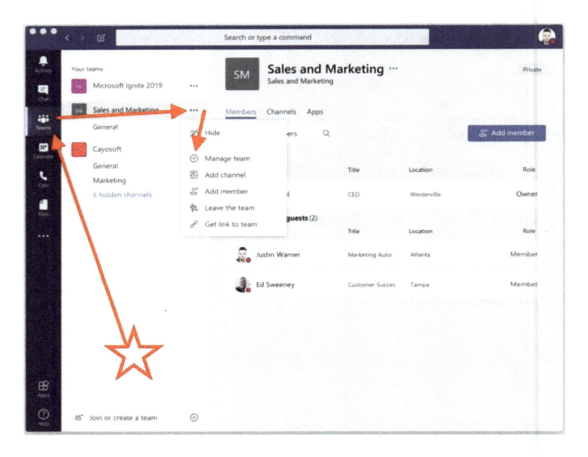

Proper role management ensures security, maintains workflow efficiency, and prevents unauthorized access.

3.4 Standard vs. Private Channels – When and How to Use Them Effectively

A Team may contain multiple Channels for different discussions, but knowing when to use **Standard** or **Private** Channels is crucial.

Standard Channels

- Visible to all members of the Team.
- Best for **general discussions, shared projects, and public resources**.
- Suitable for **company-wide announcements**.

Private Channels

- Accessible only to selected members.
- Used for **sensitive discussions, confidential projects, and limited access files**.

When to Use Each

- **Use Standard Channels** for organization-wide collaboration.
- **Use Private Channels** when discussing **HR matters, executive decisions, or confidential projects**.

Type	Who Can Join?	Use Cases
Standard	All team members	General discussions, announcements
Private	Only invited members	Confidential discussions, sensitive projects

3.5 Organizing Channels for Better Collaboration – Best Practices for Structuring Discussions

A well-organized Channel structure ensures efficient workflow. Here are best practices:

1. **Use Descriptive Names** – Avoid generic names like "General." Instead, use clear identifiers such as "Marketing Strategy" or "Product Development."
2. **Set Clear Purposes** – Define each Channel's function in the **Channel Description**.
3. **Use Channel Tabs** – Add tabs for frequently accessed files, Planner, or third-party apps.
4. **Limit the Number of Channels** – Too many Channels create clutter and confusion.
5. **Encourage Proper Tagging** – Use **@mentions** to notify specific people.

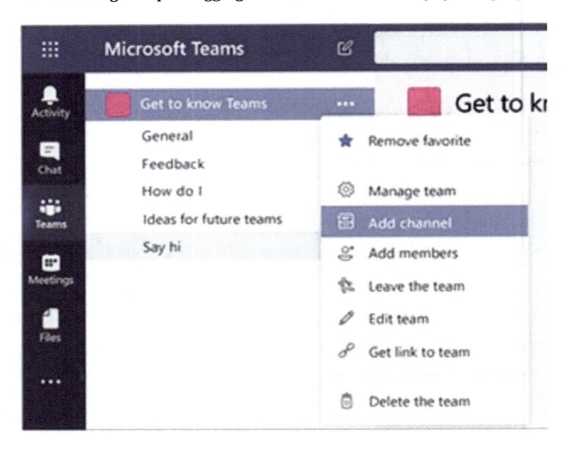

*To add channel, go to a team, click the three dots menu next to the team name, and select **Add channel.***

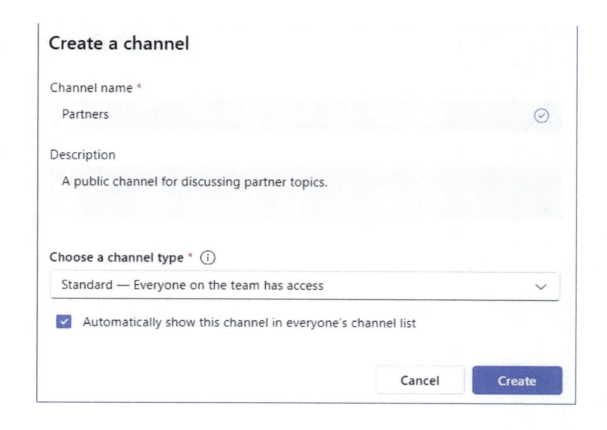

3.6 Customizing Channel Settings and Moderation – Controlling Posts and Messages

Microsoft Teams allows customization to control Channel interactions.

Customizing Settings

1. Click on the **three-dot menu** next to the Channel.
2. Select **Manage Channel**.

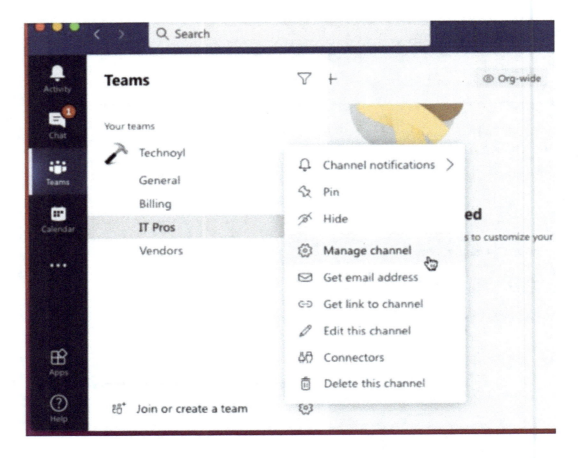

3. Modify settings such as **who can post, reply, and moderate messages**.

Using Moderation Features

- Restrict posting permissions.
- Enable message approval before posting.
- Control **@mentions and notifications**.

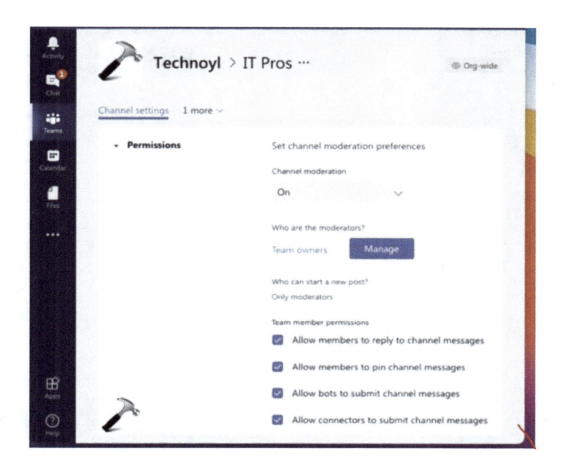

3.7 Archiving and Deleting Teams and Channels – What Happens When They Are Removed

Teams and Channels may need to be archived or deleted when no longer active.

Archiving a Team

1. Select the Team and click the three dots next to it. Select **Archive team**.
2. The Team becomes read-only.

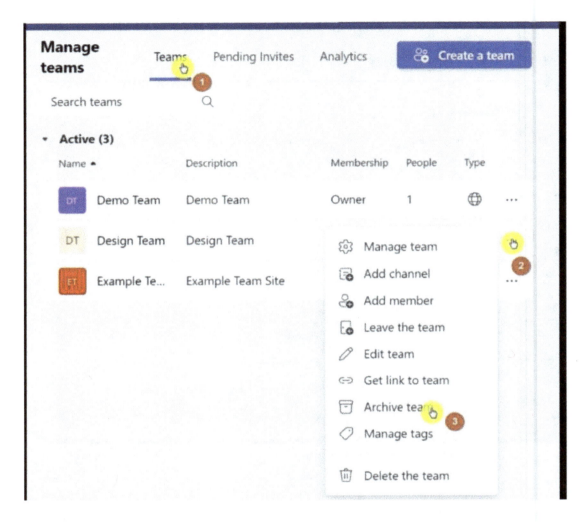

Deleting a Team or Channel

1. Open **Manage Teams** or **Manage Channel**.
2. Click **Delete Team/Channel**.
3. Confirm the action – this cannot be undone.

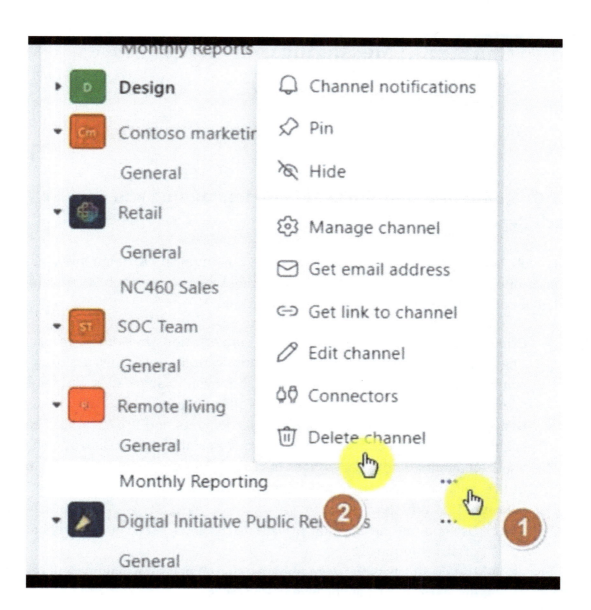

By archiving instead of deleting, important content remains accessible without cluttering active Teams.

Chapter 4: Messaging and Chat Features

4.1 One-on-One and Group Chats – Understanding When to Use Each Type

Microsoft Teams provides two primary ways to communicate through messaging: one-on-one chats and group chats. Understanding when to use each is crucial for efficient collaboration and effective communication.

- **One-on-One Chats**: These are private conversations between two users. They are best used for direct communication, quick discussions, or confidential matters. One-on-one chats allow you to share files, send voice messages, and even start video or audio calls instantly.
- **Group Chats**: These involve multiple participants and are ideal for team collaborations, project discussions, or brainstorming sessions. Group chats allow all members to see messages in real-time, share files collectively, and utilize collaborative features like mentions and reactions.
- **When to Use Which**:
    - Use one-on-one chats for private discussions, performance feedback, or direct inquiries.
    - Use group chats for team updates, shared decision-making, and open discussions on specific projects or tasks.

4.2 Starting a Conversation – Initiating Direct and Group Messages

Getting started with a chat in Microsoft Teams is straightforward. Follow these steps to start a new conversation:

- **Starting a One-on-One Chat**:
  1. Open Microsoft Teams and navigate to the **Chat** tab on the left sidebar.
  2. Click on the **New Chat** icon (represented by a pencil or '+' symbol).
  3. In the "To" field, type the name or email of the person you want to chat with.
  4. Compose your message in the text box and press **Enter** to send.

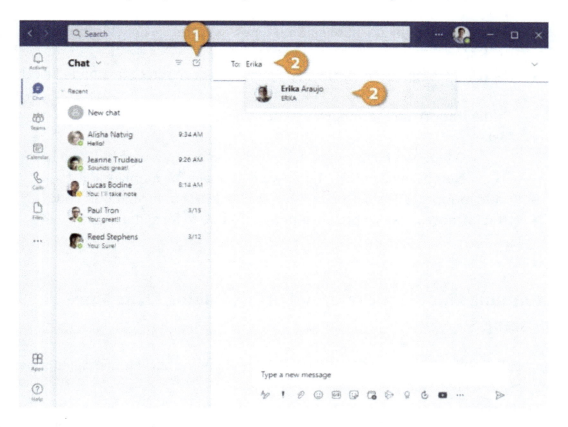

- **Starting a Group Chat**:

  1. Go to the **Chat** tab and click on the **New Chat** icon.
  2. In the "To" field, add multiple participants by typing their names or emails.
  3. Optionally, click on the down arrow beside the recipient field to name the group chat for easy identification.
  4. Write your message in the text box and press **Enter** to send.

4.3 Formatting Messages for Clarity – Using Bold, Italics, Lists, and Code Snippets

Properly formatting messages enhances readability and ensures your message is clear. Microsoft Teams provides several formatting options:

- **Bold**: To highlight key information, type **your text** or select text and click the **B** icon.
- **Italics**: To emphasize words, type *your text* or select text and click the *I* icon.
- **Underline**: To stress important words, use _your text_ or the **U** icon.
- **Lists**:
    - Bullet points: Use - or * followed by space to create bulleted lists.
    - Numbered lists: Use 1. followed by space for numbered lists.
- **Code Snippets**: Enclose text within backticks (") to format it as code.
- **Block Quotes**: Use > at the beginning of a line to format a quote.

4.4 Adding Emojis, Stickers, and GIFs – Making Chats More Engaging

Microsoft Teams allows users to add expressive elements to their messages to make conversations more engaging:

- **Emojis**: Click on the **smiley face** icon below the message box and select from various emojis.
- **Stickers**: Choose from a collection of stickers under the **Sticker** tab.
- **GIFs**: Click on the **GIF** button, search for an appropriate GIF, and insert it.

These elements can make communication more engaging and foster a positive team culture.

4.5 Using @Mentions and Alerts – Tagging Users to Get Their Attention

The **@mention** feature ensures that important messages don't go unnoticed. Here's how to use it:

- Type @ followed by the person's name to tag them in a chat.
- Use @Team to notify an entire team.
- Use @Channel to mention everyone in a specific channel.

This feature ensures that users receive notifications when they are tagged, making it useful for urgent messages.

4.6 Editing, Pinning, and Deleting Messages – Managing Past Conversations

Microsoft Teams allows users to modify messages even after sending them:

- **Editing Messages**:
    1. Hover over the message and click on the **More options (three dots)** icon.
    2. Select **Edit**, make changes, and press **Enter** to save.

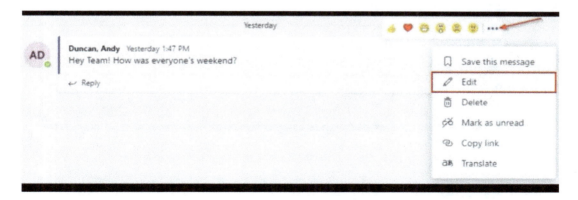

- **Pinning Messages**:

    1. Click on the **three-dot menu** of a message.
    2. Select **Pin** to keep it accessible at the top of the chat.

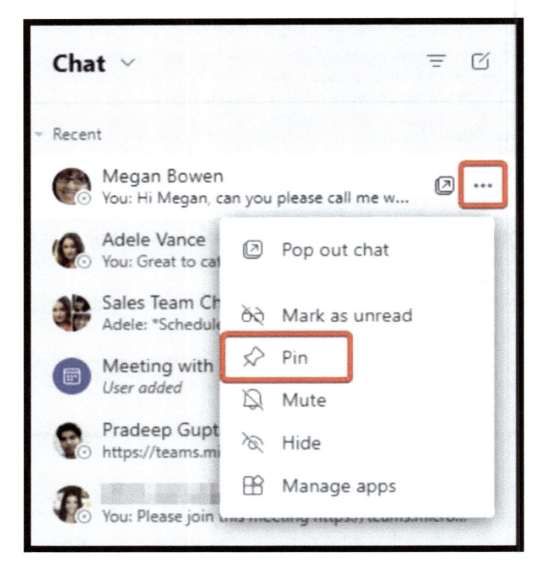

- **Deleting Messages**:

    1. Click on the **three-dot menu** next to a message.
    2. Choose **Delete** to remove it permanently.

4.7 Sending Attachments and Voice Messages – Sharing Files and Audio Efficiently

Microsoft Teams simplifies file and voice message sharing:

- **Sending Attachments**:
  1. Click the **paperclip (Attach File)** icon.
  2. Choose a file from your device, OneDrive, or a Teams channel.

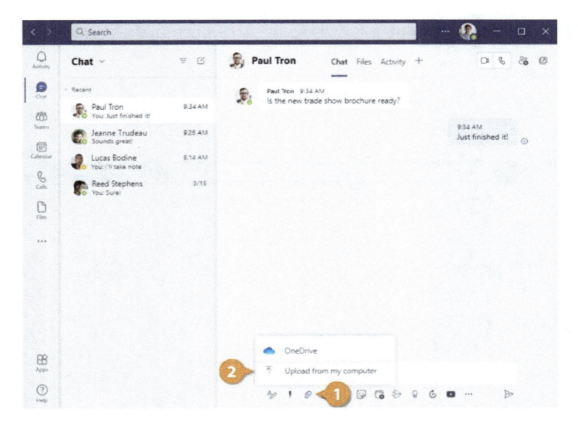

  3. Click **Send** to share.

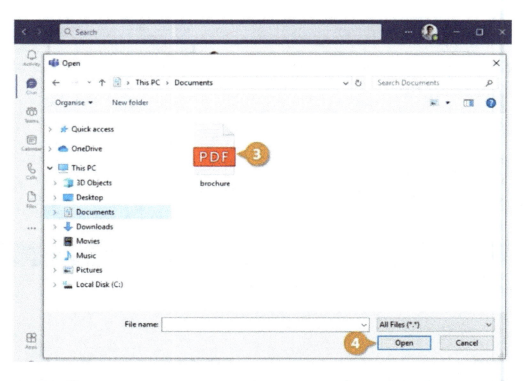

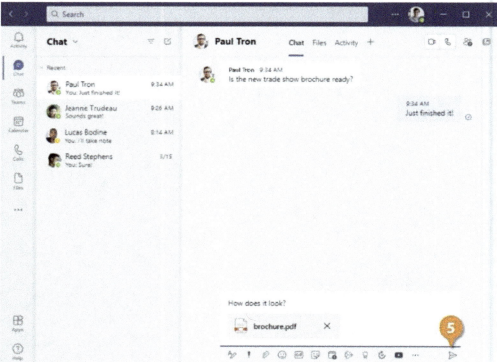

- **Sending Voice Messages**:

    1. Click the **microphone** icon in the chat box.
    2. Hold the **Record** button to capture audio.
    3. Release and click **Send** to share.

4.8 Reacting to Messages – Expressing Quick Feedback with Emoji Reactions

Message reactions allow users to quickly acknowledge or respond to a message without sending a reply:

- Hover over a message to reveal reaction options.
- Select an emoji (thumbs up, heart, laugh, surprise, sad, or angry) to react.
- Reactions provide a non-intrusive way to communicate agreement, appreciation, or other sentiments

Chapter 5: Meetings and Virtual Collaboration

5.1 How to Schedule a Meeting – Step-by-Step Instructions for Setting Up Virtual Gatherings

Microsoft Teams allows users to schedule virtual meetings in advance, ensuring structured and organized online discussions. Below is a step-by-step guide to setting up a meeting.

Understanding Meeting Scheduling in Teams

A meeting in Microsoft Teams is a planned online session where participants can discuss, collaborate, and share content in real-time. Scheduled meetings ensure that everyone is notified in advance, making it easier to plan and prepare.

Steps to Schedule a Meeting

1. **Open Microsoft Teams** – Launch the Teams application on your desktop or mobile device.
2. **Navigate to the Calendar Tab** – On the left-hand sidebar, click on **Calendar** to view available scheduling options.

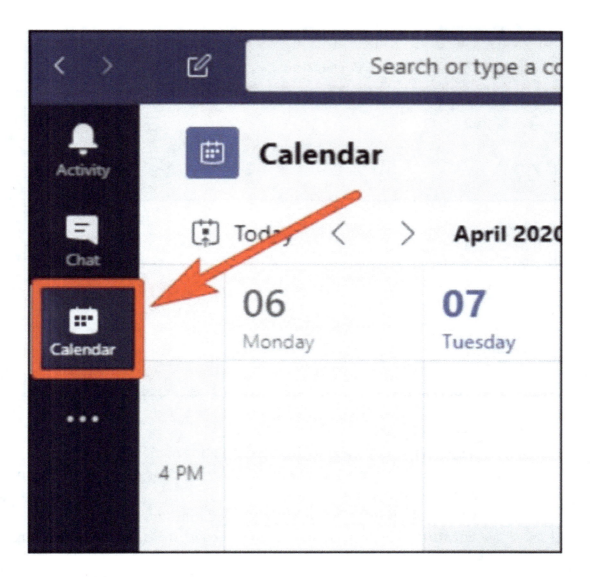

3. **Click on 'New Meeting'** – In the top-right corner, select **New Meeting** to open the meeting creation window.

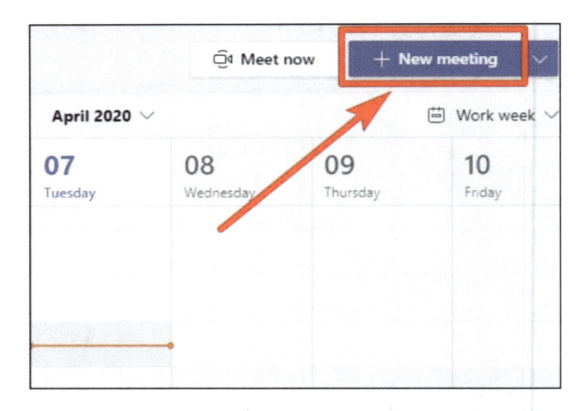

4. **Enter Meeting Details**:
   o **Title** – Provide a clear and concise meeting name.
   o **Attendees** – Add participants by entering their email addresses or selecting from contacts.
   o **Date and Time** – Choose the scheduled time and duration.
   o **Location** – For virtual meetings, leave it as 'Microsoft Teams Meeting.'
   o **Description** – Provide an agenda or important details for the meeting.
5. **Set Recurrence (Optional)** – Choose whether the meeting should repeat daily, weekly, or monthly.
6. **Configure Meeting Options** – Adjust settings such as who can bypass the lobby and who can present.
7. **Send Invitations** – Click **Save** to send invitations to all participants via email.

8. **Verify Meeting in Calendar** – Confirm that the scheduled meeting appears in your Teams calendar.

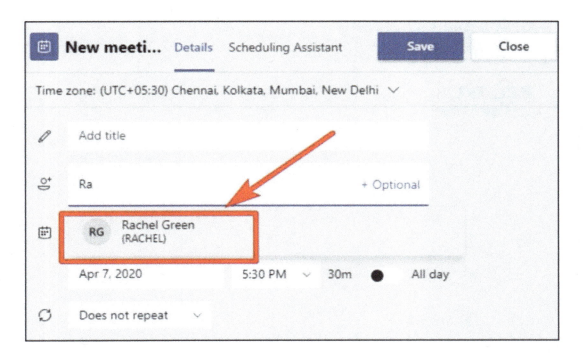

5.2 Joining a Teams Meeting – Different Ways to Access a Session

Once a meeting is scheduled, attendees can join using various methods. Here's how:

Ways to Join a Meeting

1. **Via Calendar** – Open the Teams **Calendar**, find the meeting, and click **Join**.

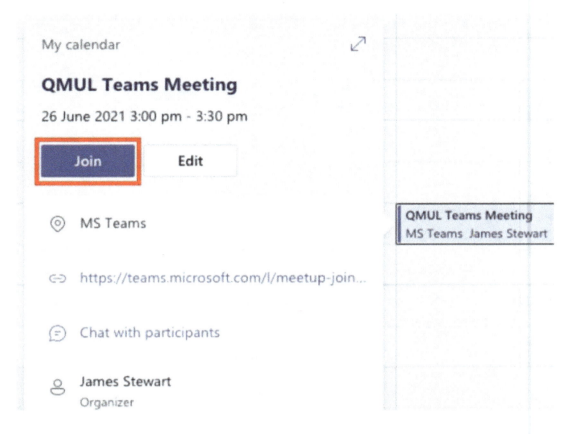

2. **From an Email Invitation** – Click on the meeting link provided in the email.
3. **Using a Meeting Link** – If someone shares a Teams meeting link, click it to access the session.
4. **Directly from a Chat** – If the meeting was created within a Teams chat, find the chat and click **Join**.
5. **By Dialing In** – If the meeting includes a phone number, dial in using a mobile or landline.
6. **Through the Teams Mobile App** – Open the app, go to **Meetings**, and tap **Join**.

5.3 Meeting Controls and Features – Managing Participants, Layouts, and Audio Settings

Microsoft Teams provides multiple in-meeting controls to enhance the user experience.

Key Meeting Controls

1. **Mute/Unmute Microphone** – Click the microphone icon to mute or unmute yourself.
2. **Turn Camera On/Off** – Click the camera icon to enable or disable video.
3. **Change Meeting Views** – Choose between **Gallery View**, **Large Gallery**, and **Together Mode** for different layouts.
4. **Manage Participants** – Click **Participants** to see who is in the meeting and mute others if needed.
5. **Adjust Audio Settings** – Open settings to switch between headset, speakers, or microphone sources.
6. **Enable Noise Suppression** – Reduce background noise by adjusting Teams' noise cancellation settings.

Main meeting controls

5.4 Assigning Roles in Meetings – Understanding Organizers, Presenters, and Attendees

Meetings in Microsoft Teams have different roles with varying permissions:

Roles in Teams Meetings

1. **Organizer** – The person who created the meeting. They can:
   - Change meeting settings
   - Assign roles
   - Start and end the meeting
2. **Presenter** – Can share screens, present content, and mute other participants.
3. **Attendee** – Can participate but has limited controls.

To assign roles:

- Click **More Options (•••)** > **Meeting Options** and adjust role settings.

5.5 Using Meeting Chat and Reactions – Engaging Without Interrupting Speakers

Using Chat Effectively

1. Click **Chat** in the meeting toolbar to open the chat panel.
2. Type messages to share notes or questions.
3. Use **@mentions** to tag participants.

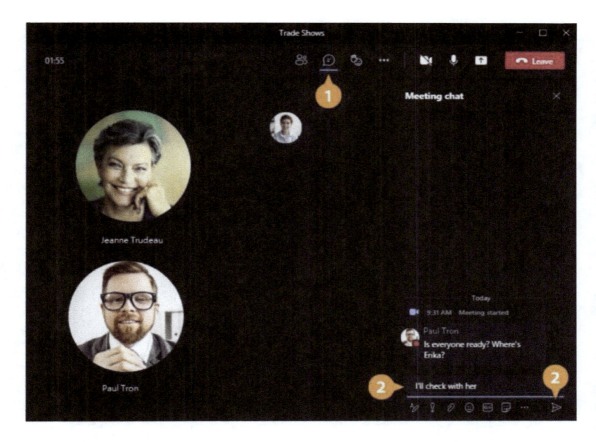

Using Reactions

1. Click the **Reactions** button.
2. Choose thumbs up, heart, clapping, or laughter to give quick feedback.

5.6 Sharing Your Screen and Presenting – Tips for Effective Online Presentations

1. Click **Share Content**.

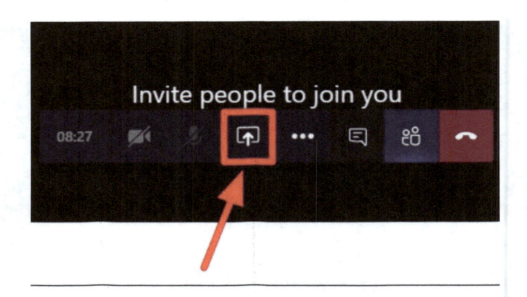

2. Choose to share a screen, window, or PowerPoint.

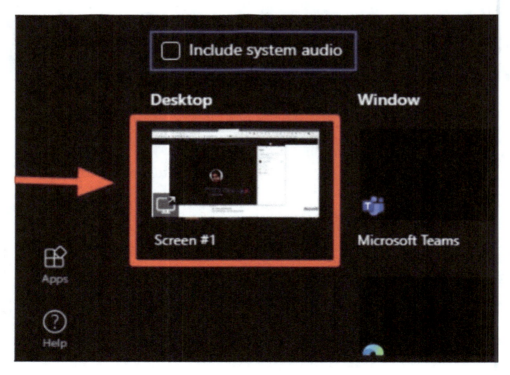

Share your full desktop screen in the meeting

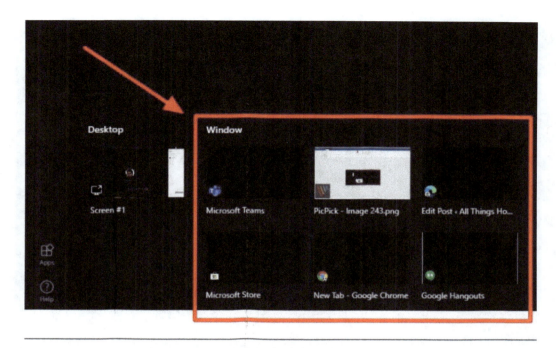

Sharing a specific window in a Microsoft Teams meeting

3. Use **Presenter Mode** to keep participants engaged.

5.7 Applying Background Effects – Using Blur and Virtual Backgrounds for a Professional Look

1. Click **More Options (•••)**.

2. Select **Apply Background Effects**.

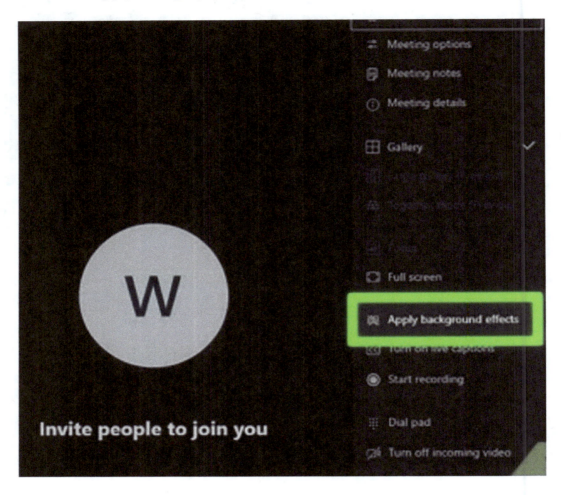

3. Choose **Blur** or upload a custom background.

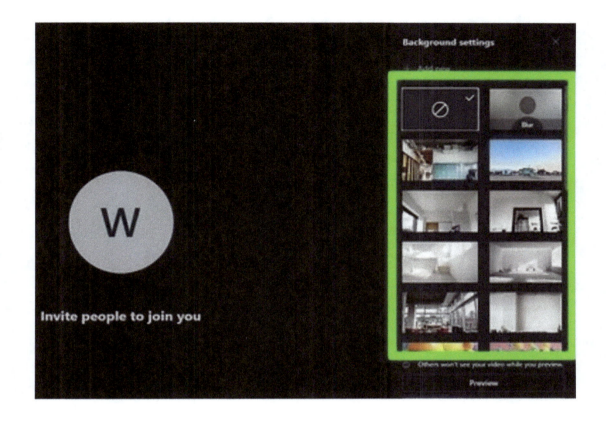

5.8 Recording a Meeting – How to Save and Access Recorded Sessions

1. Click **More Options (•••)** and select **Start Recording**.
2. Stop recording when done.
3. Access the recording in **OneDrive** or **SharePoint**.

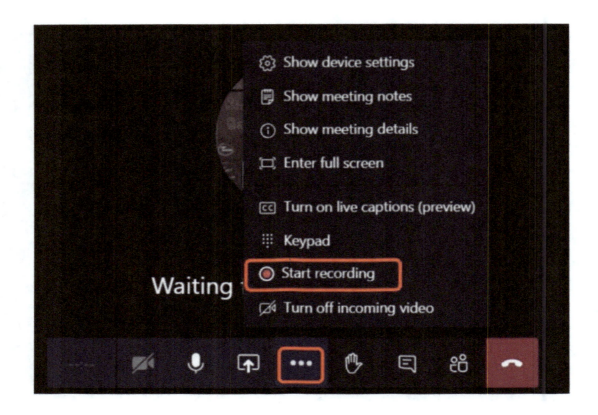

5.9 Live Captions and Subtitles – Enabling Accessibility Features for Inclusivity

1. Click **More Options (•••)**.
2. Select **Turn On Live Captions**.
3. Captions will appear at the bottom of the screen.

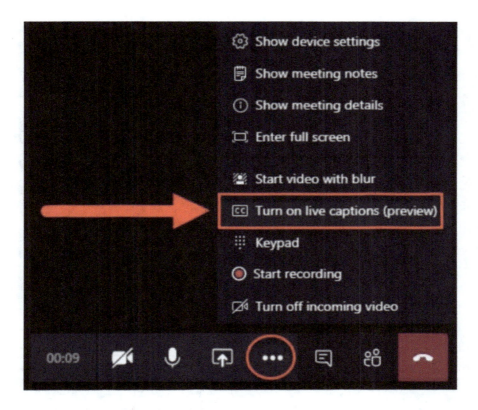

Once it's on, it will transcribe what anyone says and display it as a live caption in the lower left of the meeting screen.

Once captioning is on, as people speak, the captions appear in the bottom left.

5.10 Managing Breakout Rooms – Setting Up Smaller Discussion Groups

1. Click **Breakout Rooms**.

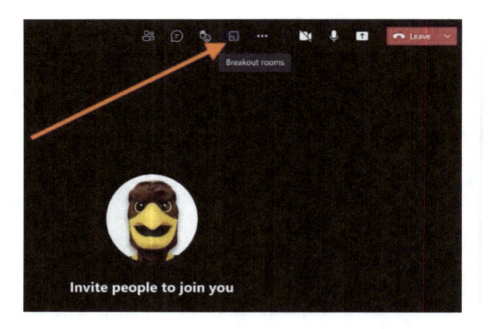

2. Choose how many rooms to create.

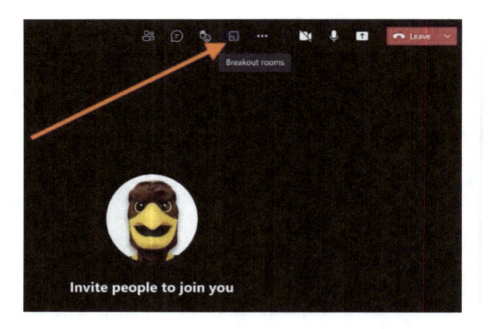

3. Assign participants manually or automatically.

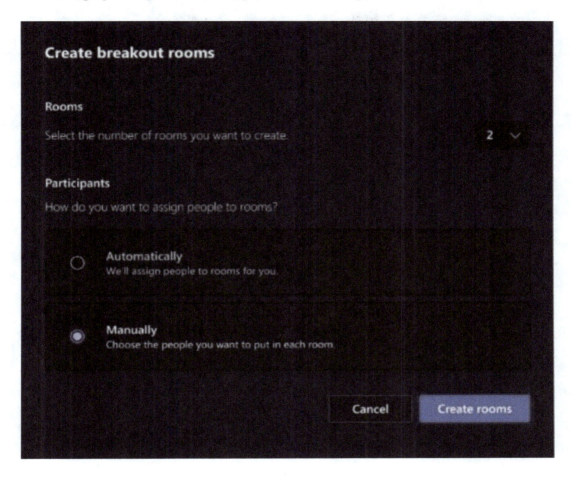

4. Click **Create Rooms** to begin discussions.

5. Close rooms when done to bring participants back to the main meeting.

Chapter 6: File Sharing and Collaborative Editing

6.1 Uploading and Sharing Documents – Drag-and-Drop, OneDrive, and SharePoint Options

Microsoft Teams provides multiple ways to upload and share documents, allowing for seamless collaboration within teams. Whether using drag-and-drop, OneDrive, or SharePoint, users can ensure that files are easily accessible to colleagues.

Understanding File Uploading and Sharing Uploading and sharing documents in Teams allows team members to work on files collaboratively without switching between different platforms. Documents can be uploaded directly to a chat, a channel, or shared through integrated cloud storage solutions such as OneDrive and SharePoint.

Methods to Upload Files

1. **Drag-and-Drop Method**
   - Open Microsoft Teams and navigate to the chat or channel where you want to upload a file.
   - Locate the file on your computer.
   - Drag the file and drop it into the message box or the Files tab within a channel.
   - Click **Send** if uploaded through chat to share it with others.
2. **Uploading via OneDrive**
   - Click on the **Attach** icon (paperclip) in a chat or channel.
   - Select **OneDrive** from the options.

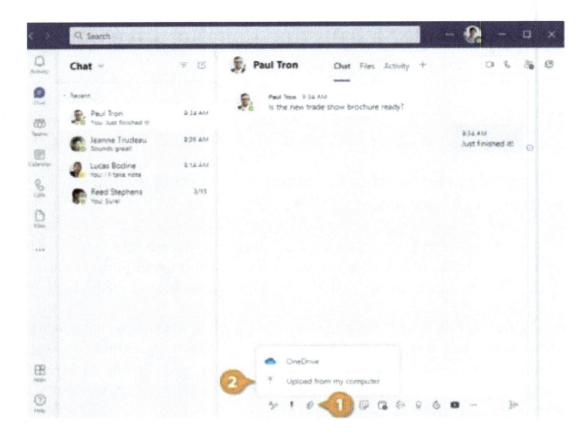

- o Browse for the document you want to share.
- o Select the file and click **Share**.
- o Adjust permissions as needed before sharing.

3. **Uploading via SharePoint**
   - o Go to the **Files** tab of the respective channel.
   - o Click **Upload**, then select **Files** or **Folder**.
   - o Browse and select the document.
   - o The file is stored in the SharePoint document library linked to the channel.

Adjusting File Permissions When sharing a document, users can modify access levels:

- **Can edit**: Allows recipients to make changes to the document.
- **Can view**: Recipients can only read the document without modifying it.

- **Specific people**: Restricts access to selected individuals.

6.2 Real-Time Co-Authoring – Collaborating on Word, Excel, and PowerPoint Simultaneously

Real-time co-authoring allows multiple users to edit documents simultaneously while viewing each other's changes live. This feature improves productivity and eliminates the need for back-and-forth email exchanges.

How Real-Time Co-Authoring Works

1. **Open the File in Microsoft Teams**
   - Navigate to the **Files** tab within a chat or channel.
   - Click on the document you want to edit.
   - Select **Open in Teams**, **Open in Browser**, or **Open in Desktop App**.
2. **Collaborate with Team Members**
   - As users edit the document, changes appear instantly.
   - Each collaborator's cursor is marked with their name.
   - Use the **Comments** section to leave notes for team members.
3. **Save and Track Changes**
   - Microsoft Teams automatically saves changes.
   - Version history allows you to track modifications and revert if needed.

6.3 Recovering Previous Versions – Understanding Document History and Restoring Files

Microsoft Teams stores document history, allowing users to recover older versions of files. This is crucial for undoing mistakes or retrieving important content.

Accessing Version History

1. Locate the document in Teams.
2. Click on the **More Options** (three dots) next to the file.

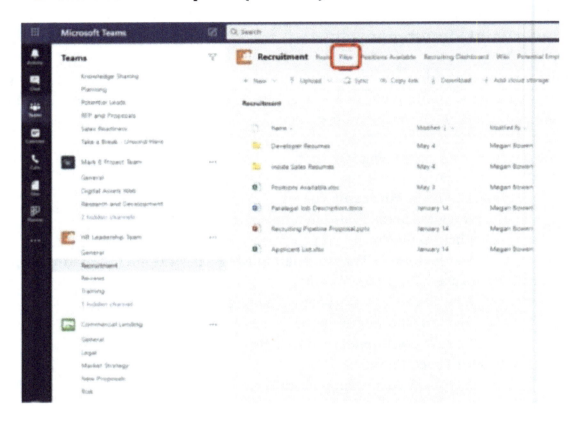

3. Select **Open in SharePoint**.
4. In SharePoint, click **Version History**.
5. Browse and select the version you want to restore.

Restoring a Previous Version

- Click **Restore** to replace the current version with an earlier one.
- Click **Download** to keep a copy before making changes.

6.4 Managing Files Within Teams – Organizing Shared Content in Channels

Organizing files efficiently within Teams prevents clutter and makes document retrieval easier.

Best Practices for Managing Files

1. **Use Folders to Categorize Documents**
   - Within a channel's **Files** tab, click **New > Folder**.
   - Name the folder and move relevant files into it.
2. **Pin Important Files**
   - Click on the file and select **Pin to Top**.
   - This keeps essential files easily accessible.
3. **Use Metadata and Tags**
   - Apply labels and tags to categorize documents based on projects or topics.
4. **Set File Permissions Properly**
   - Restrict access to sensitive documents using SharePoint permissions.

6.5 Synchronizing Files with OneDrive – Ensuring Accessibility Across All Devices

Syncing Teams files with OneDrive allows users to access documents from multiple devices, including mobile phones and tablets.

Steps to Sync Files with OneDrive

1. Open Teams and navigate to the **Files** tab.
2. Click on **Open in SharePoint**.
3. In SharePoint, click **Sync** (this will prompt OneDrive setup if not already configured).
4. Follow on-screen instructions to sync folders to your local device.

Benefits of Syncing Files

- Enables offline access to important documents.
- Keeps files updated across all devices.
- Provides backup and recovery options.

Chapter 7: Enhancing Productivity with Apps and Tools

7.1 Using Microsoft Planner and To-Do – Task Management for Better Workflow

Microsoft Planner and Microsoft To-Do are powerful task management tools integrated into Microsoft Teams. They help users organize tasks, improve collaboration, and streamline workflow by keeping track of assignments and deadlines.

Understanding Microsoft Planner

Microsoft Planner is a team-based task management tool that allows users to create plans, assign tasks, track progress, and collaborate within Teams. It is designed for project management and teamwork.

Features and Benefits of Microsoft Planner:

1. **Task Organization** – Break down work into tasks, assign responsibilities, and set due dates.
2. **Visual Task Management** – Use Kanban boards with buckets for easy task organization.
3. **Collaboration Tools** – Attach files, comment on tasks, and update statuses in real-time.
4. **Integration with Microsoft 365** – Syncs with Outlook and Teams for seamless task tracking.
5. **Task Filtering and Search** – Quickly find and manage tasks using filters and labels.

Using Microsoft Planner in Teams (Step-by-Step Guide):

1. **Open Microsoft Teams** and go to the desired **Team** where you want to create a Planner.
2. **Click on the "+" button** in the top menu to add a new tab.
3. **Search for "Planner"** and select the Microsoft Planner app.

4. **Choose "Create a new plan"** or add an existing plan to the Team.

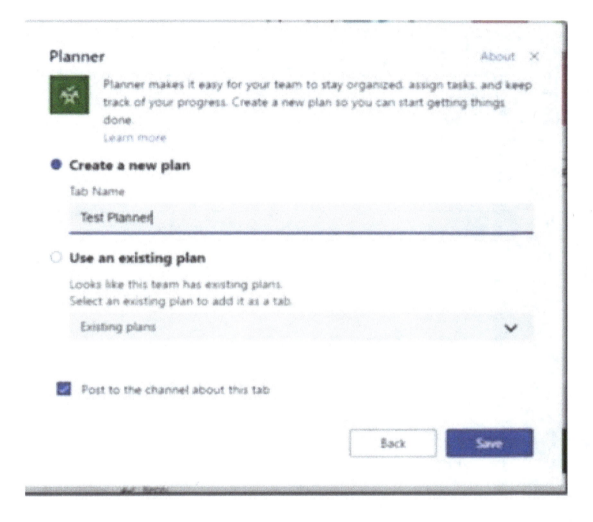

5. **Name the plan** and click "Save" to add it as a tab in Teams.
6. **Create tasks** by clicking "Add task," entering task details, setting due dates, and assigning owners.

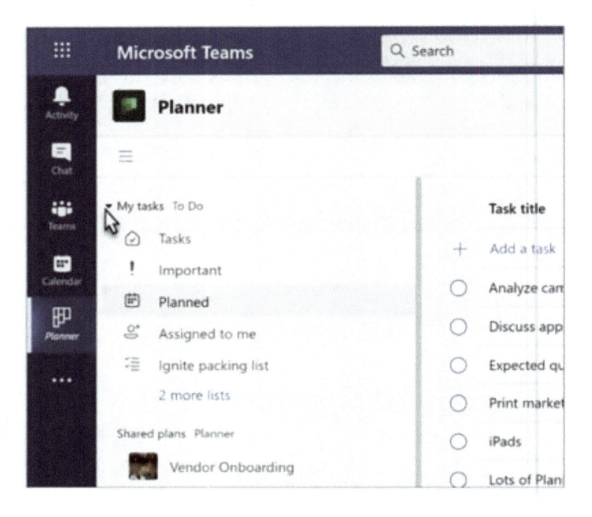

7. **Organize tasks** into different buckets for better structure.
8. **Update task progress** by marking them as "Not started," "In progress," or "Completed."
9. **Use charts and schedule views** to track team progress visually.

Understanding Microsoft To-Do

Microsoft To-Do is a personal task management tool designed for individual users to manage daily tasks and reminders.

Features and Benefits of Microsoft To-Do:

1. **Daily Task List** – Create and prioritize daily tasks.

2. **Reminders and Notifications** – Get notified of upcoming deadlines.
3. **Task Categorization** – Organize tasks into lists and folders.
4. **Integration with Outlook** – Syncs seamlessly with Outlook Tasks.
5. **Cross-Device Access** – Access tasks on Windows, Mac, iOS, and Android.

Using Microsoft To-Do (Step-by-Step Guide):

1. **Open Microsoft To-Do** on your browser or download the app.
2. **Sign in with your Microsoft account.**
3. **Click "New List"** to create a categorized task list.
4. **Add tasks** by clicking on "Add a task."
5. **Set due dates and reminders** to keep track of important tasks.
6. **Mark tasks as completed** when finished.
7. **Use "My Day"** to focus on daily priority tasks.

7.2 Integrating Third-Party Applications – Adding Trello, Asana, Zoom, and Other Tools

Microsoft Teams supports third-party app integrations, allowing users to enhance collaboration and productivity by connecting external tools like Trello, Asana, and Zoom.

Benefits of Integrating Third-Party Apps in Teams:

1. **Centralized Workspace** – Access all tools within Teams.
2. **Enhanced Productivity** – Streamline workflows without switching apps.
3. **Seamless Collaboration** – Integrate project management and communication tools.

How to Add Third-Party Apps to Microsoft Teams (Step-by-Step Guide):

1. **Open Microsoft Teams** and navigate to the left-hand sidebar.
2. **Click on "Apps"** at the bottom of the sidebar.
3. **Search for the app** you want to integrate (e.g., Trello, Asana, Zoom).

4. **Select the app** and click "Add."
5. **Follow the setup instructions** to connect the app to Teams.
6. **Access the app** from the left-hand sidebar or within team channels.

7.3 Creating and Managing Surveys – Collecting Feedback Efficiently Using Microsoft Forms

Microsoft Forms allows users to create surveys, quizzes, and polls to collect feedback.

Benefits of Using Microsoft Forms:

1. **Easy Survey Creation** – Create surveys with different question types.
2. **Real-Time Responses** – Get instant feedback and data analysis.
3. **Seamless Integration with Teams** – Share forms in chats and channels.

Creating a Survey in Microsoft Forms (Step-by-Step Guide):

1. **Open Microsoft Forms** in your browser.

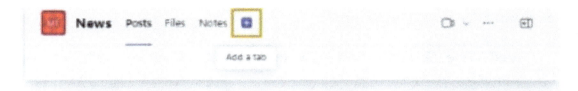

Find the Microsoft Forms app and click it:

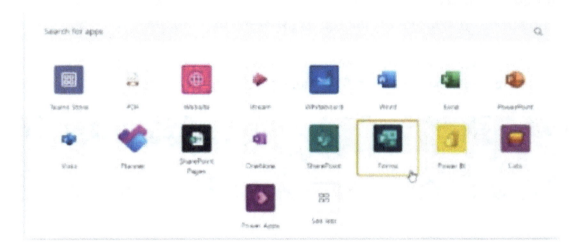

2. **Click "New Form."**
3. **Add questions** by selecting different formats (multiple choice, text, rating, etc.).
4. **Customize settings** like required responses and response limits.
5. **Share the survey link** via Teams or email.
6. **View responses** in real-time under the "Responses" tab.

7.4 Using Whiteboard for Visual Collaboration – Brainstorming Ideas in Meetings

Microsoft Whiteboard is a digital canvas for brainstorming and collaboration.

Benefits of Microsoft Whiteboard:

1. **Real-Time Collaboration** – Team members can draw, write, and edit simultaneously.
2. **Supports Multiple Devices** – Accessible on PCs, tablets, and smartphones.
3. **Integration with Teams Meetings** – Used for visual brainstorming in meetings.

Using Microsoft Whiteboard in Teams (Step-by-Step Guide):

1. **Open Microsoft Teams** and join a meeting.
2. **Click on "Share Content"** and select "Microsoft Whiteboard."

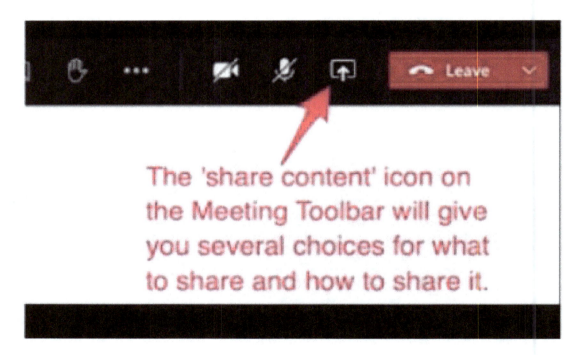

3. **Start drawing and adding notes** using the provided tools.

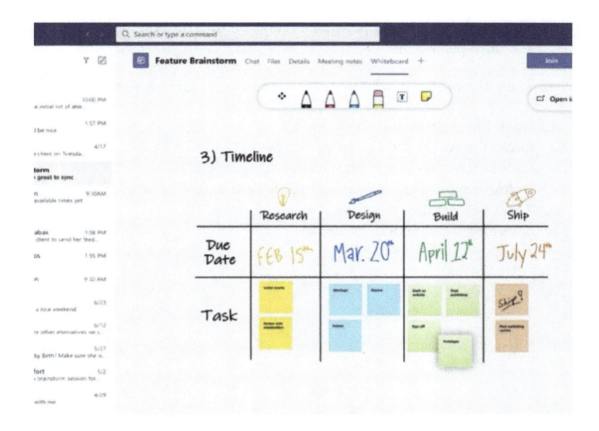

4. **Invite participants** to collaborate on the Whiteboard.
5. **Save the Whiteboard session** for later reference.

7.5 Automating Workflows with Power Automate – Enhancing Efficiency Through Automation

Microsoft Power Automate allows users to create automated workflows to reduce manual tasks.

Benefits of Power Automate:

1. **Saves Time** – Automates repetitive tasks.
2. **Improves Accuracy** – Reduces human errors in workflows.

3. **Integrates with Multiple Apps** – Works with Teams, Outlook, SharePoint, and third-party tools.

Creating an Automated Workflow in Power Automate (Step-by-Step Guide):

1. **Open Power Automate** and sign in.
2. **Click "Create"** to start a new workflow.
3. **Choose a trigger** (e.g., "When a new email arrives").
4. **Define actions** (e.g., "Save email attachment to OneDrive").
5. **Test the workflow** to ensure it functions correctly.
6. **Save and activate** the automation.

Chapter 8: Security, Privacy, and Administrative Controls

8.1 Managing Permissions and Access – Assigning Appropriate Roles and Restrictions

Managing permissions and access control in Microsoft Teams ensures that users have the appropriate level of authority and access to information without compromising security. Microsoft Teams uses a role-based structure to regulate access within teams and channels.

1. Understanding Roles in Microsoft Teams

Microsoft Teams offers different roles that dictate the level of access and control each user has:

- **Owner**: The creator of the team or an assigned administrator. Owners can add or remove members, assign roles, manage settings, and delete the team.
- **Member**: Regular participants who can send messages, collaborate on files, and access resources within the team.
- **Guest**: External users who have limited access to the team's resources and can be restricted from certain features.

2. Assigning Roles and Managing Permissions

To ensure the correct users have the right permissions:

- Open **Microsoft Teams** and navigate to the team you want to manage.
- Click on **More options (...)** next to the team name and select **Manage team**.

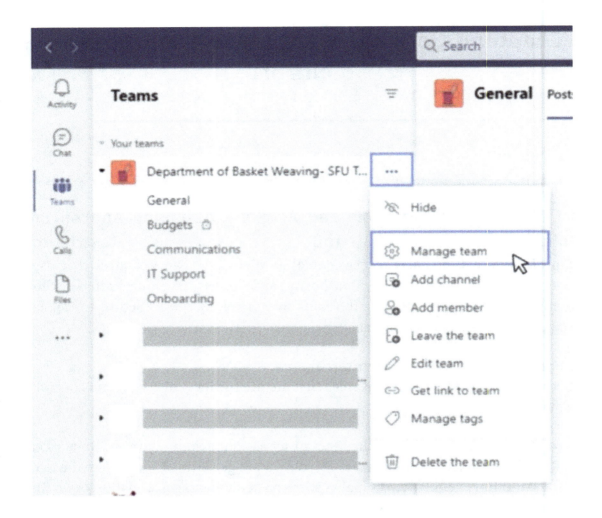

- In the **Members** tab, locate the user whose role you want to change.
- Click the **dropdown menu** next to their name and select **Owner**, **Member**, or **Guest**.
- To remove a user, click on the **Remove** option next to their name.

3. Setting Channel Permissions

- Go to the specific **channel** in the team.
- Click on **More options (...) > Manage channel**.
- Adjust the settings to control who can post, reply, or moderate the content.
- Private channels can be created for sensitive discussions, allowing only selected members access.

8.2 Adding External Collaborators – Securely Working with Guests and Outside Users

External collaboration in Microsoft Teams allows businesses and organizations to work with people outside their organization while ensuring data security.

1. Enabling Guest Access in Microsoft Teams

Before adding external users, ensure that **guest access** is enabled:

- Open **Microsoft Teams Admin Center**.
- Navigate to **Org-wide settings > Guest access**.
- Toggle the switch to **Allow guest access in Teams**.
- Configure additional guest permissions such as calling, messaging, and screen sharing.

2. Inviting an External User to a Team

- Open **Microsoft Teams** and go to the **team** where you want to add an external user.
- Click on **More options (...) > Add member**.
- Enter the **email address** of the external collaborator.
- Microsoft Teams will recognize that the user is outside the organization and prompt you to add them as a **Guest**.
- Click **Add**, then customize their permissions as needed.

3. Managing Guest Permissions

- Go to the **Teams settings**.
- Click on **Manage team > Settings > Guest permissions**.
- Enable or restrict features such as file sharing, messaging, and adding channels.

4. Best Practices for Secure Collaboration with External Users

- Use **Private Channels** to restrict sensitive conversations.

- Limit guests from accessing **shared files** unless necessary.
- Enable **auditing logs** to track external activity.

8.3 Enabling Two-Factor Authentication – Strengthening Account Security

Two-Factor Authentication (2FA) adds an extra layer of security by requiring a second form of verification in addition to a password.

1. Enabling Two-Factor Authentication in Microsoft Teams

To activate 2FA for Microsoft Teams:

- Go to the **Microsoft 365 Admin Center**.
- Navigate to **Users > Active users**.
- Select the user(s) for whom you want to enable 2FA.
- Click on **Manage multi-factor authentication**.
- Select the user and click **Enable**.
- Click on **Enforce** to make it mandatory for login.

2. Setting Up Two-Factor Authentication for Users

- After 2FA is enabled, users must set it up during their next login.
- On the login screen, they will be prompted to configure 2FA.
- They can choose one of the following verification methods:
  - **Authenticator App** (Microsoft Authenticator, Google Authenticator)
  - **SMS Code**
  - **Phone Call**
- Follow the on-screen steps to complete the setup.

3. Best Practices for Using 2FA Securely

- Use **Authenticator Apps** instead of SMS where possible, as SMS-based 2FA can be vulnerable to phishing attacks.
- Regularly **review and update** 2FA settings.

- If a user loses access to their 2FA method, an administrator can reset it in the **Admin Center**.

8.4 Data Security and Compliance – Understanding Microsoft Teams' Security Policies

Microsoft Teams adheres to strict security protocols to protect user data, prevent unauthorized access, and ensure compliance with industry regulations.

1. Microsoft Teams Security Features

- **Data Encryption**: All data in Microsoft Teams is encrypted at rest and in transit.
- **Secure Access Controls**: Users must authenticate using Microsoft 365 credentials.
- **Compliance with Standards**: Microsoft Teams meets industry regulations such as **GDPR, ISO 27001, HIPAA, and SOC 2**.

2. Setting Up Data Loss Prevention (DLP) Policies

To prevent unauthorized data sharing:

- Open **Microsoft 365 Compliance Center**.
- Navigate to **Data Loss Prevention**.
- Create a **New Policy** and specify the data types to protect (financial, health, personal data).
- Define actions (block, notify, allow override) for users attempting to share sensitive data.

3. Enabling Sensitivity Labels in Microsoft Teams

- Go to **Microsoft 365 Security & Compliance Center**.
- Under **Classification > Sensitivity labels**, create a new label.
- Configure settings for data encryption, access restrictions, and external sharing limitations.
- Apply labels to **Teams, SharePoint, and OneDrive**.

4. Auditing and Monitoring Activity

- Open **Microsoft Purview Compliance Portal**.
- Under **Audit**, enable **Log Recording** to track activity.
- Regularly review reports to identify potential security threats.

5. Compliance and Regulatory Standards

- **HIPAA**: Protects health-related data in healthcare organizations.
- **GDPR**: Ensures data privacy for users in the European Union.
- **ISO 27001**: Certifies information security management.

Chapter 9: Microsoft Teams for Different Users and Industries

---

9.1 Teams for Business Use – Streamlining Communication Across an Organization

Understanding Microsoft Teams for Business

Microsoft Teams is a powerful communication and collaboration tool that enables businesses to streamline workflows, enhance productivity, and centralize team communication. It allows employees to collaborate in real time, share files, conduct virtual meetings, and integrate with various business applications within the Microsoft 365 ecosystem.

Why Businesses Use Microsoft Teams

1. **Centralized Communication** – Teams serve as a hub for messages, calls, and meetings, reducing reliance on emails.
2. **Enhanced Collaboration** – Employees can work together in real-time on documents using Microsoft Word, Excel, and PowerPoint.
3. **Improved Productivity** – Features like task management, file sharing, and workflow automation make teamwork more efficient.
4. **Integration with Business Tools** – Supports third-party apps like Trello, Asana, Slack, and CRM tools for better workflow management.
5. **Security and Compliance** – Enterprise-level security ensures data protection and compliance with industry regulations.

Key Features for Businesses

1. **Teams and Channels** – Organize departments or projects into dedicated spaces for structured discussions.
2. **Meetings and Video Conferencing** – Conduct high-quality virtual meetings with recording, live captions, and screen sharing.
3. **Task and Workflow Management** – Utilize Microsoft Planner, To-Do, and Power Automate to assign and track tasks.
4. **File Sharing and Co-Authoring** – Store and collaborate on documents using OneDrive and SharePoint integration.
5. **Guest Access and External Collaboration** – Work with clients, vendors, and stakeholders securely.

How to Set Up Microsoft Teams for a Business

1. **Sign Up for Microsoft Teams Business** – Choose a suitable Microsoft 365 plan and create an account.
2. **Set Up Teams and Channels** – Organize workspaces for departments, projects, or initiatives.
3. **Add Team Members and Assign Roles** – Manage permissions by assigning owners, members, and guests.
4. **Configure Security and Compliance Settings** – Enable data encryption, multi-factor authentication, and access controls.
5. **Integrate Business Applications** – Connect CRM, project management, and analytics tools to enhance efficiency.
6. **Train Employees and Encourage Adoption** – Provide tutorials and best practices for seamless onboarding.

9.2 Teams in Education – Utilizing the Platform for Virtual Classrooms and Assignments

Understanding Microsoft Teams for Education

Microsoft Teams for Education is designed to create a seamless digital learning environment, allowing educators to conduct classes, assign work, provide feedback, and engage with students in a collaborative space. It helps facilitate both in-person and remote learning.

Why Schools and Universities Use Microsoft Teams

1. **Virtual Classrooms** – Conduct live lessons, record lectures, and engage students with interactive tools.
2. **Assignments and Grading** – Assign, collect, and grade student work digitally.
3. **Collaboration Between Teachers and Students** – Chat, video call, and co-edit documents in real time.
4. **Integration with Learning Management Systems (LMS)** – Supports Moodle, Blackboard, and other LMS tools.
5. **Secure Learning Environment** – Protects student data and ensures compliance with educational privacy laws.

Key Features for Educators and Students

1. **Class Teams and Channels** – Organize classes by subject, grade, or project for structured communication.
2. **Assignments and Homework Management** – Upload assignments, set deadlines, and provide feedback in one place.
3. **Live Classes and Meetings** – Conduct online lectures, one-on-one sessions, or group discussions.
4. **Shared Notebooks with OneNote** – Keep track of lesson plans, student notes, and collaborative work.
5. **Parent and Guardian Access** – Keep parents informed about student progress and assignments.

How to Use Microsoft Teams for Education

1. **Sign Up for Microsoft Teams for Education** – Schools can set up free or premium accounts through Microsoft 365.
2. **Create a Class Team** – Set up classes with designated students and educators.
3. **Schedule Virtual Classes** – Use the calendar feature to schedule live sessions with students.
4. **Assign and Grade Work** – Upload assignments, provide instructions, and review submissions.
5. **Encourage Student Engagement** – Use chat, polls, quizzes, and discussion boards to make learning interactive.
6. **Monitor Student Performance** – Track participation, grades, and progress through built-in analytics.

9.3 Teams in Healthcare – Supporting Patient Communication and Telemedicine

Understanding Microsoft Teams for Healthcare

Microsoft Teams is increasingly being used in the healthcare industry to support secure communication, telemedicine, and collaboration between healthcare professionals. It allows doctors, nurses, and medical staff to coordinate patient care efficiently.

Why Healthcare Institutions Use Microsoft Teams

1. **Telemedicine and Virtual Consultations** – Enables remote patient appointments with secure video conferencing.
2. **HIPAA and GDPR Compliance** – Ensures patient data is protected according to healthcare regulations.
3. **Secure Messaging Between Staff** – Allows encrypted communication for discussing patient cases.

4. **Integration with Electronic Health Records (EHR)** – Syncs with systems like Epic and Cerner for seamless patient management.
5. **Crisis Response Coordination** – Helps healthcare teams respond quickly to emergencies and critical situations.

Key Features for Healthcare Providers

1. **Virtual Visits** – Conduct online patient consultations with secure video and audio calls.
2. **Secure Messaging and File Sharing** – Share patient reports, lab results, and treatment plans securely.
3. **On-Call Scheduling and Coordination** – Manage shifts, patient rounds, and emergency response teams.
4. **AI-Powered Chatbots for Patient Support** – Automate appointment booking and basic inquiries.
5. **Remote Collaboration for Medical Teams** – Connect doctors, nurses, and specialists across locations.

How to Implement Microsoft Teams in Healthcare

1. **Set Up a Microsoft Teams Healthcare Account** – Ensure compliance with healthcare data privacy regulations.
2. **Create Dedicated Teams for Departments** – Organize teams based on hospital departments or specializations.
3. **Integrate with EHR Systems** – Connect with electronic medical records for seamless access to patient data.
4. **Enable Virtual Patient Consultations** – Set up secure video conferencing tools for telehealth.
5. **Train Healthcare Staff** – Provide training on how to use Teams securely and effectively in a medical setting.

9.4 Teams for Personal Use – Staying Connected with Family and Friends

Understanding Microsoft Teams for Personal Use

While Microsoft Teams is widely known for business and education, it also serves as a valuable platform for personal communication. It helps families and friends stay connected through video calls, group chats, and file sharing.

Why Individuals Use Microsoft Teams

1. **Free and Secure Communication** – Allows unlimited messaging, calling, and file sharing.
2. **Virtual Family Gatherings** – Host video calls with loved ones, even across different locations.
3. **Event Planning and Coordination** – Plan birthdays, reunions, and other events using shared calendars and lists.
4. **Collaborative Projects** – Work on shared documents, whether for family history projects or community activities.
5. **Cross-Platform Accessibility** – Use on mobile, desktop, and web browsers for seamless connectivity.

Key Features for Personal Use

1. **Group Chats and Video Calls** – Stay in touch with family and friends through instant messaging and meetings.
2. **File and Photo Sharing** – Share photos, videos, and documents in a private space.
3. **Shared To-Do Lists and Calendars** – Organize family schedules and reminders.
4. **Private and Secure Conversations** – Protect personal data with encryption.

How to Use Microsoft Teams for Personal Communication

1. **Sign Up for a Free Microsoft Teams Account** – Create a personal account using an email or phone number.
2. **Create a Family or Friends Group** – Set up a private team for ongoing conversations.
3. **Schedule Virtual Meetups** – Use the calendar to organize virtual gatherings.
4. **Share Photos and Documents** – Upload and store memories in a shared space.

Chapter 10: Expert Tips, Troubleshooting, and Advanced Features

---

10.1 Time-Saving Keyboard Shortcuts – Speeding Up Tasks with Quick Commands

Microsoft Teams includes several keyboard shortcuts that can help you navigate the interface faster and perform tasks efficiently without relying on a mouse. By mastering these shortcuts, users can save time, improve workflow, and enhance productivity.

10.1.1 What Are Keyboard Shortcuts?

Keyboard shortcuts are combinations of keys that execute specific functions within an application. Instead of manually clicking through menus, shortcuts allow users to perform tasks quickly. These shortcuts enhance accessibility and enable seamless multitasking.

10.1.2 Benefits of Using Keyboard Shortcuts

- **Efficiency:** Reduces the number of clicks required to perform tasks.
- **Speed:** Helps users navigate Teams faster.
- **Convenience:** Makes it easier to work without switching between a mouse and keyboard.
- **Accessibility:** Beneficial for users who have difficulty using a mouse.

10.1.3 Essential Keyboard Shortcuts in Microsoft Teams
Navigation Shortcuts

- **Ctrl + 1, 2, 3, etc. (Windows) / Command + 1, 2, 3, etc. (Mac)** - Switch between different sections like Activity, Chat, Teams, and Calendar.
- **Ctrl + E (Windows) / Command + E (Mac)** - Quickly access the search bar.
- **Ctrl + , (Windows) / Command + , (Mac)** - Open settings.

Messaging Shortcuts

- **Ctrl + N (Windows) / Command + N (Mac)** - Start a new chat.
- **Ctrl + Enter (Windows) / Command + Enter (Mac)** - Send a message without pressing the send button.
- **Ctrl + Shift + X (Windows) / Command + Shift + X (Mac)** - Expand the compose box for formatting options.

Call and Meeting Shortcuts

- **Ctrl + Shift + M (Windows) / Command + Shift + M (Mac)** - Mute/unmute microphone.
- **Ctrl + Shift + O (Windows) / Command + Shift + O (Mac)** - Turn camera on/off.
- **Ctrl + Shift + K (Windows) / Command + Shift + K (Mac)** - Raise/lower hand during a meeting.

File and Navigation Shortcuts

- **Ctrl + Shift + F (Windows) / Command + Shift + F (Mac)** - Open the search bar.
- **Ctrl + O (Windows) / Command + O (Mac)** - Attach a file to a message.

10.1.4 How to Memorize and Practice Keyboard Shortcuts

1. **Start with the most used shortcuts:** Focus on navigation and messaging shortcuts first.

2. **Use shortcut cheat sheets:** Print a list of shortcuts and keep it near your workstation.
3. **Practice regularly:** Implement shortcuts in daily activities to build muscle memory.
4. **Enable shortcut reminders:** Some versions of Teams provide tips when using the mouse.

10.2 Hidden Features and Smart Tips – Little-Known Tricks to Improve Efficiency

10.2.1 Introduction to Hidden Features

Beyond the common functions, Microsoft Teams includes various hidden features that can significantly improve productivity and streamline workflows. These lesser-known tools can enhance the overall user experience.

10.2.2 Useful Hidden Features in Microsoft Teams
1. Slash Commands

Users can type "/" in the search bar to see available commands, such as:

- **/unread** - Show all unread messages.
- **/mentions** - Display recent mentions.
- **/available** - Change status to Available.

2. Bookmarking Messages

To save important messages for later reference:

- Hover over the message and click "**...**".
- Select **"Save this message"**.
- Access saved messages by typing **/saved** in the search bar.

3. Pinning Chats and Channels

- Right-click on a chat or channel.
- Select **"Pin"** to keep it at the top.

4. Message Translation

- Click on a received message in another language.
- Select **"Translate"** to convert it to your preferred language.

5. *Meeting Recap and Transcription*

After a meeting:

- Navigate to the meeting chat.
- Access the **transcript and summary**.

10.3 Common Problems and Fixes – Resolving Connectivity, Audio, and Video Issues

Microsoft Teams users may encounter various issues, such as connectivity problems, microphone malfunctions, or video glitches. Understanding common troubleshooting steps can help resolve these problems quickly.

10.3.1 Troubleshooting Connection Issues
1. Check Your Internet Connection

- Restart your router or switch to a wired connection.
- Run a speed test to ensure your network meets the minimum bandwidth requirement.

2. Restart Microsoft Teams

- Close and reopen Teams.
- Log out and log back in.

3. Clear Cache and Update Teams

- Navigate to **C:\Users[YourName]\AppData\Roaming\Microsoft\Teams** and delete cache files.
- Update Microsoft Teams via **Settings > About Teams > Check for updates**.

10.3.2 Fixing Audio and Microphone Issues

- Ensure the correct microphone is selected in **Settings > Devices**.
- Check **Windows Sound Settings** to see if Teams is muted.

10.3.3 Solving Video Problems

- Verify the camera is enabled in **Settings > Devices**.
- Restart Teams or reinstall the app.

10.4 Customizing Notifications – Reducing Distractions While Staying Informed

Microsoft Teams allows users to customize notifications to reduce distractions while staying informed about important updates.

10.4.1 Adjusting Notification Settings

- Go to **Settings > Notifications**.
- Customize alerts for chats, mentions, and activity.

10.4.2 Managing Channel Notifications

- Click the **"..."** next to a channel.
- Select **"Channel notifications"** and adjust preferences.

10.5 Using Teams on Mobile Devices – Optimizing the App on Smartphones and Tablets

10.5.1 Downloading and Installing Teams on Mobile

- Visit the **App Store (iOS)** or **Google Play Store (Android)**.
- Download and install Microsoft Teams.

10.5.2 Optimizing Mobile Experience

- Enable **Push Notifications** for instant updates.
- Use **Dark Mode** to reduce eye strain.

10.6 Staying Updated with New Features – Keeping Up with the Latest Microsoft Teams Enhancements

10.6.1 How to Check for Updates

- Open Teams and go to **Settings > About Teams > Check for updates**.

10.6.2 Enabling Preview Features

- Turn on **Public Preview Mode** in **Settings > About Teams** to access early releases.

10.6.3 Following Microsoft Teams Announcements

- Visit the **Microsoft Teams Blog** for feature releases.
- Join the **Microsoft Tech Community** to discuss updates.

Index

www.ingramcontent.com/pod-product-compliance
Lightning Source LLC
LaVergne TN
LVHW080118070326

832902LV00015B/2651